BOURNVILL
Steam & Chocolate

By Mike Hitches

Cadbury No.6 0-4-0 loco, built by Avonside Engine Company of Bristol in 1922, outside the company's locoshed. (Roger Carpenter Collection)

IRWELL PRESS

Copyright Irwell Press, Mike Hitches
First Published 1992
Reprinted 1996
ISBN 1-871608-31-7

An early advertisement for Cadbury's Cocoa, one of the products of the famous Bournville works which was transported by the Midland Railway. (Cadbury Ltd)

Published by Irwell Press
PO Box 1260, Caernarfon, Gwynedd, LL55 3ZD
Printed by the Amadeus Press
Huddersfield West Yorkshire

INTRODUCTION

Bournville is world-renowned both for chocolate from Cadbury's factory and a great social experiment that was to revolutionise the type of housing built for 'working class' people. What is little known, is the part that the siting of the railway and little station played in this story. Without these two, it is very unlikely that any of these developments would have taken place. The railways were central to the rapid transport of raw materials and finished products. Any plans for a factory at a given location would depend on the proximity of suitable railway connections.

Establishment of the Birmingham West Suburban Railway, with its eventual connection to the rest of the national system, and the building of a station near a 'green field' site at Bournbrook made the area suitable for new industry and it was a particularly ideal location for the production of foodstuffs. Once Cadbury had established their factory and village, the population increased to meet the demand for labour, as the company expanded its operations. Cadbury established its own substantial railway within the factory complex, to facilitate the distribution of raw material and to remove finished goods, this being connected to the main line system. Growth was such that the works railway warranted its own engine shed.

This book attempts to tell the story of the station and railway at Bournville, their part in the industrial and social development of the area, and their relationship to the West Suburban Line in this small area of Birmingham.

A portrait of George Cadbury who, with his brother Richard, established the works at Bournville and went on to build the garden village. (Cadbury Ltd).

Cadbury No.6 loco on the works railway. In the background are vans used to transport chocolate products on the main line. (R.C. Riley)

Cadbury's first steam loco, an 0-4-0 saddle tank, hauls a mixed train of Midland Railway and the company's own wagons around the works. In the background is the main Birmingham West Suburban Line and the tunnel carrying the main line and Birmingham and Worcester Canal over Bournville Lane. (Cadbury Ltd)

One of Cadbury's Avonside built locos hauls a train of chocolate products up towards the warehouse at 'Waterside' on the opposite bank of the Birmingham and Worcester Canal. Coal wagons, whose loads are to be used in the factory and on the company's engine, are on the left and the factory lies in the background. (Cadbury Ltd)

THE BIRMINGHAM AND GLOUCESTER RAILWAY

Bournville station came into existence as an indirect result of the engineering of the Birmingham and Gloucester Railway. The establishment of this railway allowed for the later development of the Birmingham West Suburban Line, on which Bournville station stands.

A line from Birmingham to Bristol was first mooted by the Sturge Brothers, a Quaker family with industrial interests in Birmingham, to encourage the rapid development of industry in the West Midlands, and to link up with the major port of Bristol. The Sturge Company still has a factory at Lifford.

Brunel was employed by the Sturges to survey the line, but investment in the project was slow and it languished. Had the line been built, it is almost certain that it would have been broad gauge and the later 'battle of the gauges' at Gloucester may never have happened when it did, although the matter would have had to be resolved eventually and, who knows, it may have been in favour of 7ft. ¼n. instead of 4ft.8¹/¹²n., with profound effects elsewhere.

The 'battle of the gauges' started at the point where the Birmingham and Gloucester railway met the broad gauge of the Bristol and Gloucester railway. This meant that goods had to be transferred from the wagons of one company onto those of the other. The same applied to passengers who were forced to change onto different carriages to complete their journeys. By the mid 1850s the broad gauge was faltering and the narrow gauge was spreading apace.

A few years after Brunel's survey, Captain William Scarth Moorsom, brother of the future Chairman of the LNWR, surveyed a new route which took a line from Birmingham to Gloucester, a port on the River Severn, avoiding Worcester, Droitwich and Tewkesbury, which all opposed the railway. Cheltenham wanted it and the town prospered thereby.

The Birmingham and Gloucester Railway Bill passed through Parliament at the first attempt through a careful choice of route, but it did include the famous Lickey Bank, a fearful gradient of 1 in 37. The line from Birmingham to Cheltenham opened in 1840 from a temporary terminus at Camp Hill, Birmingham and as a planned junction with other Birmingham lines, it was built to the standard gauge. Trains eventually terminated at the Curzon Street station of the London and Birmingham Railway.

The line to Camp Hill passes the St. Andrews ground of Birmingham City Football Club. There is a story that every Saturday afternoon an old goods train used to pass behind the ground shrouding the railway end with engine smoke. If Birmingham City were attacking that end the ball would always be in the back of the net when the smoke cleared. Whether there is any truth in this tale is open to question but the club has never been as successful since steam disappeared from this section of the line.

In January 1845, the Bristol and Gloucester Railway, a standard gauge line incorporated by Act of Parliament in 1839 and using an old tramway from Coalpit Heath to Bristol and the Birmingham and Gloucester Railway were amalgamated, to form the Birmingham and Bristol Railway. This completed the link between the West Midlands and the major port, which the original protagonists had visualised.

Amalgamation of the two companies stimulated the interest of the Great Western Railway who wanted to take over the B&B in order to bring the broad gauge into Birmingham at Curzon Street, right into the heart of narrow gauge territory. The London and Birmingham Railway was the champion of 4ft. 8½in. as the standard for Britain's railway network and introducing the broad gauge would throw a 'spanner in the works'. In order to put this into effect, the GWR offered £60 for every £100 B&B share. The B&B held out for £65. Meanwhile, John Ellis, Deputy Chairman of the Midland Railway, met Edmund Sturge and Joseph Gibbons, two Directors of the B&B on a train to London, and in typical Midland 'wheeling and dealing' fashion, offered better terms than the GWR, securing the B&B for the Midland Railway and 'narrow gauge' interests.

Loss of the B&B to the Midland meant that the GWR had to improve its own line from Birmingham to Bristol in order to compete. Its original line had run via Worcester, Hereford and the Severn tunnel; a distance of 133 miles with an alternative via Didcot and Banbury (141 miles). By the turn of the century, the company had completed a new route via Honeybourne and Cheltenham, reducing this distance to 95 miles. The GWR was also forced to spend a considerable amount of money over the years on the expansion of their own main station at Snow Hill, instead of having access to New Street once it had opened. The LNWR were relieved that the Midland had bought the B&B, which had prevented the GWR having access to New Street, for the two companies had never really 'got on'. In appreciation of this, the Midland was readily given access to New Street after it opened on 1st June 1854. The Midland Railway continued to use Curzon Street until 30th June when portions of expresses were detached at Camp Hill for New Street. A few weeks later, all trains terminated at the new station.

THE BIRMINGHAM WEST SUBURBAN LINE

The existence of the Birmingham and Gloucester Railway between Camp Hill and Kings Norton, gave the impetus for providing a branch line to run west of a junction at Lifford to Birmingham. Private promoters received authorisation for a single line branch from Albion Wharf in central Birmingham, to Lifford on 31st July 1871. The Birmingham West Suburban Railway Company started work on the branch soon afterwards. Plans were altered as construction was underway and the line was terminated at Granville Street, in order to avoid the expense of bridging the Birmingham and Worcester Canal.

During construction, the Midland Railway obtained authorisation, on 30th July 1874, for

Bournville railway station, c.1904, shortly after '& Stirchley Street' was dropped from its title. (Lens of Sutton)

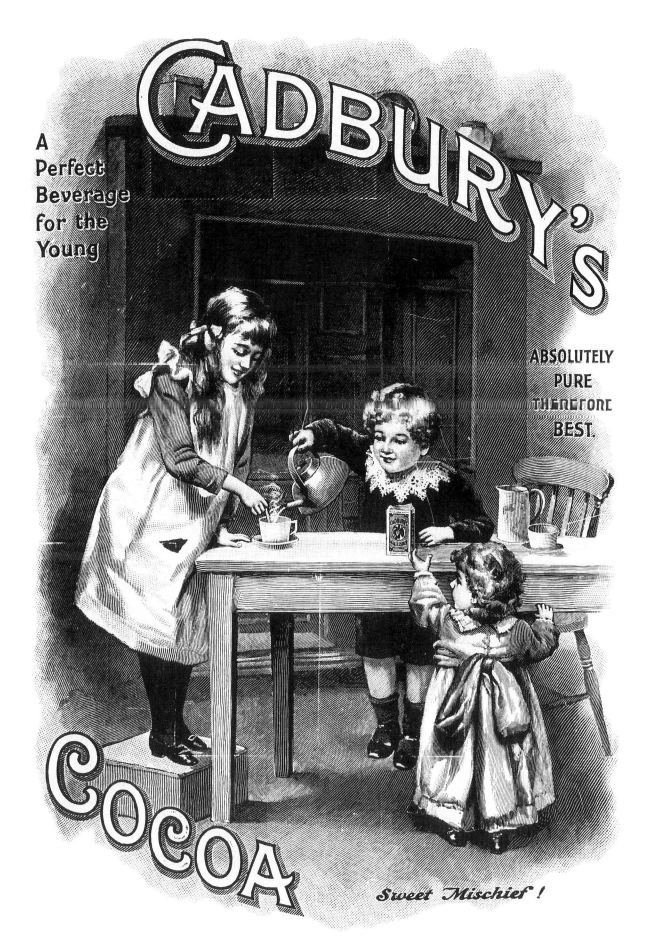

Sweet Mischief! One of the attractive Edwardian advertisements for Cadbury's Cocoa. Transport of Bournville's products brought substantial revenue to the Midland Railway. (Cadbury Ltd)

a branch to the canal at Lifford, thus making a junction with the main line. On 1st July 1875, the Birmingham West Suburban became part of the Midland Railway itself. On 3rd April 1876, it opened as a single line with stations at Church Road, Somerset Road, Selly Oak, which had a passing loop, and Stirchley Street. A station was opened at Lifford on 1st June. All local trains, worked by the Midland, ran to Kings Norton.

Very soon after opening, the Midland Railway gave thought to extending the line into New Street. An Act of 18th July 1881 authorised doubling the line and a connection to Church Road, near Granville Street, forming a junction. The Granville Street terminus was to be closed and replaced by a new station at Five Ways. The contractor, Joseph Firbank, began work in 1883, and in order to gain access to New Street station three tunnels, 225 yards, 184 yards and 88 yards, and cuttings and embankments were necessary. One embankment alone meant the removal of 120,000 cubic yards of soil. 1,100 men were employed on the project, along with 60 horses, 7 locomotives, 7 steam cranes and 10 portable engines. While all this was going on, the canal, which was 70 feet above the level of New Street station, had to be carried on wooden troughs, being fully restored when the railway earthworks were complete.

Work was completed in 1885 and expresses were re-routed along the BWSR on 1st October of that year. At the same time the Midland extension of New Street station was completed, enabling the company to have the use of its own platforms. The line was double to Stirchley Street; the section between Church Road and Granville Street was extended to give access to a central goods depot opened by the Midland on 1st July 1887, on the opposite bank of the canal. The original BWSR plan was to bridge the waterway at this point to reach Worcester Wharf, the title of the depot until 1892. The Midland decided to tunnel underneath at a gradient of 1 in 80.

From Stirchley Street, a more direct line was constructed to Kings Norton; opening on 26th September 1885 it eliminated the junction with the main line at Lifford, which became a short branch, with the station re-sited on the Gloucester line. A triangle was completed at Lifford in 1892, giving suburban services a circular route. The extension to Kings Norton allowed direct connection with the original Birmingham and Gloucester main line and allowed the original Camp Hill section to be downgraded to a suburban branch as the BWSR became the new main line, a status it still retains today.

The Camp Hill branch is now only used for freight traffic, or as a passenger through route avoiding New Street when required. The retention of this section for freight proved useful as a connection with the big Lawley Street goods depot, avoiding congested New Street. Suburban passenger traffic ceased on the line on the 27th January 1941 with the closure of Brighton Road, Moseley (which suffered bomb damage) and Kings Heath, as a wartime measure. With no demand for reopening after the war, closures were finally confirmed on 27th November 1946.

Construction of the BWSR appears to have been inevitable once the Midland Railway had an established base at New Street, being a more direct route to link Derby, headquarters of the company, and Bristol than the more circuitous line via Camp Hill. It is a distinct possibility that it would have been built as a main line from the first if the Midland had control straight away; its branch status in any event only lasted nine years. This being the case, then it is quite likely that fewer stations would have been established along the route, or in different locations, meaning that there may not have been one at Bournville. Had the line been developed later, Cadbury may not have established their chocolate factory in the area and the world famous name may never have been coined.

EARLY YEARS AT BOURNVILLE STATION

As part of the development of the Birmingham West Suburban Railway, a new station was opened, adjacent to the Birmingham and Worcester Canal, in the undeveloped fields near to Bournbrook, on 3rd April 1876. The station was intended to serve the population of the nearby district of Stirchley, a quarter of a mile east of the railway, and was named 'Stirchley Street', the title by which the area was known at this time. This was the original 'Bournville' station, though it was to undergo a few name changes first.

The Cadbury family established their new chocolate factory just west of the station in 1879 and gave the area its name of Bournville shortly afterwards. This was incorporated into the station name on 4th March 1880 when it was retitled 'Stirchley Street and Bournville'.

The later Bournville Village, creating an increased population and demand for trains, reflected the growing importance of the district to the BWSR. As if to illustrate the influence and importance of this new development, the Midland Railway reversed the station name to 'Bournville and Stirchley Street' in July 1888.

In April 1904 'Stirchley Street' was dropped and the station became simply

A pair of Cadbury saddle tank locos with their trains at the 'Waterside' warehouse. The horse and cart in the centre is loaded with empty churns, the milk having been used for 'Dairy Milk' chocolate.

A view of Bournville station in Midland Railway days, from the Mary Vale Road overbridge. A Kirtley 0-6-0 tender engine arrives at the station with a local train for Kings Norton. (Lens of Sutton)

A Johnson 275 Class 0-6-0 3F goods engine brings empty stock into Bournville station, which will then take Cadbury's employees for a day at the seaside, during the summer of 1912. Flat caps and straw boaters are fashionable headgear of the day. How many of the men in this view would still be alive to take advantage of these trips in six years time? This picture was taken from the subway entrance to the down side of the station and clearly shows the narrow platform, small cantilever waiting shelter and Midland Railway station nameboard. (Cadbury Ltd)

'Bournville', a title it has retained ever since. It was built on an embankment, as was the canal at this point. Access was from below via a concourse at street level where a brick building, with wooden canopy, housed the ticket office, booking hall and parcels office, the platform being reached by staircase with two flights of stairs. The station entrance was, and still is, situated at Bournville Lane, opposite Cadbury's works, and just a few yards west of a low, narrow tunnel, only wide enough to allow one vehicle at a time, which passes under the railway and canal, just north of the station. This tunnel links Bournville and Stirchley and because of tight clearances, the number 27 bus service from West Heath to Kings Heath via Bournville Lane has always been operated by single deckers. From the 1950s to the mid-1960s these vehicles were narrow bodied Leyland Tigers and a small number of Leyland Olympics with a seating capacity of about 25. By the late 1960s, the service was operated by single deck versions of rear engined Daimler Fleetlines with larger seating capacity. This was the only such service, using single-deck vehicles, operating in Birmingham for a number of years.

When opened, the railway was only a single line branch, thus only one platform was required. Buildings on the platform consisted of separate single storey waiting room and station masters house. The buildings were of blue brick to the dampcourse, the rest red brick with two bands (one third and two thirds height) of white glazed brick. The whole was topped by hipped slate roofs, with decorative stonework at the top of the walls, and two tall chimneys to each building. The platform was protected by a pair of deep, heavy wooden canopies supported on plain cast iron brackets. Lighting was typical Midland Railway gas lamps, and standard Midland signalling was used in the locality of the station. The buildings were typical of the Midland Railway, which was very conscious of passenger comfort, and they were almost certainly designed by John Sidney Crossley, engineer in chief of the Midland who had been responsible for the 'house style' since his appointment in 1858.

Doubling of the track on the BWSR in 1885 meant that a narrow platform had to built opposite the original one between the railway and canal, with access by subway from the main concourse at street level, through the embankment and up steps, protected by a shelter on the platform. Lack of space on this new platform, through the presence of the canal, produced a small cantilever waiting shelter of very modest proportions. This, of course, meant that no footbridge has ever been built on the station. There was another entrance to the station; down steps from the Mary Vale Road overbridge, which went out of use in the 1970s. When opened, Bournville had a resident station master who was,

according to the census of 1881, a Mr. Edwin Brownett, who had come from Bibury, Gloucestershire along with his wife and five children. Also resident were his father in law, who was a night watchman, and a nephew who was a railway porter. These were almost certainly the only staff on the station. Another 1885 development was the building of a more direct line from the station to Kings Norton, the original being converted for use as a siding.

The single line branch saw only local traffic when first opened, but after doubling and the connection with New Street, expresses from Derby to Bristol used the BWSR as the more direct route than the Camp Hill line. The local services were quite intensive, following Midland policy of light, frequent trains, and services from New Street to Kings Norton, Redditch and Ashchurch, used both the Camp Hill line and the BWSR. Once the Lifford curve had been completed in 1892, a circular service, utilising both lines, came into operation, making Bournville a junction with lines to Kings Norton and Lifford. The BWSR also carried a local service to Halesowen via Northfield with five trains each way on weekdays. Virtually all of these local services called at Bournville.

A wet day marks the very first railway excursion to see Cadbury's works, organised by the LMS. Interest in seeing how chocolate is made seems to have attracted a full train. Trips to the works proved very popular and many thousands of people arrived at Bournville station over the years to view the famous works. The loco which hauled this train is a Johnson Class 3 4-4-0. The proximity of the Birmingham and Worcester Canal explains why the down platform at the station is so narrow. (National Railway Museum)

Centrepiece of the Bournville Village is the village green, seen here in springtime, judging by blooming crocus; the resthouse is in the centre, and the junior and infant school complete with tower which contains a carillon of bells. (Bournville Village Trust)

Almshouses in Mary Vale Road, at the edge of Bournville Village, good examples of the architectural style used. (Bournville Village Trust)

Passengers using the station numbered around 120,000 a year, the development of Cadbury's works and the Bournville village increasing loadings to a peak of 201,324 in 1900. From then on, there was a downturn in numbers and by 1905 only 128,483 passengers were booked. Season ticket holders, however, increased from 80 in 1896 to 604 in 1904. Parcels receipts showed a steady increase from £2729 in 1896 to £4851 in 1904.

Much of the motive power for all of this traffic was supplied by Saltley shed, until Bournville's own roundhouse opened in 1895, in the hope that traffic would expand still further. That it did not was largely due to the fact that the City of Birmingham was always going to be more concerned with road transport than rail. Once the tram system had been developed in the City, good services would be available on the A38, Bristol Road, at nearby Selly Oak and, even closer, at Stirchley – all went to the City centre and the new outer suburbs. This was also the City of the bicycle, motor cycle and, perhaps even more important, the motor car. There were motor cycle and bicycle manufacturers in Selly Oak as well as the renowned BSA works at Small Heath.

Herbert Austin was to open his famous car factory at Longbridge, two miles south of Bournville in 1905, his first vehicle coming off the production line in 1906. The population of the Bournville area would, in future, look principally to road transport to serve their needs.

Freight traffic through Bournville consisted of local pick-up goods until the establishment of the Cadbury factory, which demanded the rail shipment of raw materials in bulk. Further increases came when the central goods depot opened in 1887, attracting traffic to and from the West of England. Trains used the BWSR to reach that depot, though the premises at Lawley Street, developed when Curzon Street station closed, would always be more important, its traffic going via the Camp Hill line.

By the time the station acquired the title 'Bournville' Cadbury's chocolate factory and the new village were well established. The BWSR now enjoyed main line status with express trains passing through, along with intensive local passenger services. Freight traffic was burgeoning and passenger figures showed that a station here had proved worth-

while. Its future looked promising.

CADBURY AND THE BOURNVILLE VILLAGE

The decision to establish a chocolate factory in the district south of Bournbrook was taken by brothers Richard and George Cadbury, members of a Birmingham Quaker family, in 1879. Their father, John, had already set up a tea and coffee shop in Bull Street in the centre of town, in 1824. A few years later, he established a cocoa and chocolate business in Bridge Street, handing it over to his sons in 1861.

Their factory was becoming too small and there was also a need for clean air and water, something not readily available in the centre of a large Victorian town. Being Quakers, they were also concerned for the condition of their workers. The rural area of Bournbrook, named after a local stream, was ideal because the firm would be in the country, yet only four miles from the town centre. There was good air and a plentiful supply of clean water from the Bourn. Another important factor was the proximity of the Birmingham and Worcester

Canal and the newly developed Birmingham West Suburban line for the transport of their chocolate products.

Early in 1879 the first bricks were laid for the new factory and it was finished in late summer of the same year. The area about was renamed Bournville, for at this time it was considered that the best food came from France; the new name would give the company a French 'feel' which the Cadburys considered would be good for sales. So it proved to be and anyone who has ever eaten chocolate has heard of Bournville even if they have never seen the place.

George Cadbury determined he would try to do something to improve the lives of the 'labouring classes' and Bournville was to become synonymous with a pioneering scheme of workers' housing, providing a model for many other undertakings throughout Great Britain. Like his father, George Cadbury held strong beliefs and had been concerned, for many years, at the terrible conditions and bad housing of the 'deserving poor' in the industrial cities. Many of the Cadbury workforce lived in dismal squalor and, along with his brother, and other Quakers, George made frequent visits to the slums in efforts to alleviate the worst effects of the conditions in which these people lived. The opportunity to 'do something' presented itself when the company moved to Bournbrook. While the factory was under construction, sixteen cottages, providing a standard of accommodation vastly superior to anything available anywhere else in Birmingham, were built for the key workers of the new factory.

Once the new factory had become established, George Cadbury could devote more time toward fulfilling his dream of providing good quality housing for the working classes. In the early 1890s he started to purchase land near to the factory; by 1895 he had bought 120 acres, sufficient to start building. Alexander Harvey was engaged as architect with instructions that houses should be of a certain size and that there should be variations of style to prevent the endless terraces which characterised 'artisan' districts. Gardens should not be less than one-sixth of an acre and they should all have at least six fruit trees so that families could be self sufficient in fruit and vegetables – regarded with some prescience by George as a vital part of a family's diet. Finally each house was to cost *not less* than £150 to build. The land was laid out as the 'Bournville Building Estate' and it was inspired by a model village in County Armagh, Ulster, called Bessbrook and built by yet another Quaker family, the Richardsons, who were linen manufacturers.

A total of 143 houses were built in the first Bournville development and some were sold for £200 each, purchased over 15 years on mortgages of 2½% to people who could pay a deposit of £50. Others were let to tenants and it is interesting to note that less than half of the houses were occupied by employees of Cadbury. It was always the intention that the estate should not be let wholly to the

The Friends Meeting House on Bournville Village Green. As the Cadbury family were Quakers, a meeting house was an essential structure here. (Bournville Village Trust)

The Village Green with the meeting house on the right and Ruskin Hall, which was an Art College, on the left. (Bournville Village Trust)

Sycamore Road, Bournville, with the War Memorial on the green. (Bournville Village Trust)

The Shopping Parade on Sycamore Road, Bournville. It appears that Cadbury's are not afraid of competition, judging by the 'Rowntrees' van parked behind the car. (Bournville Village Trust)

firm's employees, but it should be open to anyone who wished to live there.

In order to prevent speculative building in the area, and to allow for expansion of the village later on, George Cadbury decided to form a Trust and thereby relinquish all financial interest himself. The estate would be run by twelve trustees, nine from the Cadbury family and the others drawn from the new City of Birmingham, University of Birmingham, and the Society of Friends. On the 14th December 1900 the Bournville Village Trust was formed, its duties to administer the village for the benefit of its residents and to prevent exploitation of the area by builders and property developers.

The clean environment and spacious housing soon brought improvements in the health of the inhabitants and within a few years, the infant mortality rate was around seven per thousand in Bournville compared to an average of thirteen per thousand for the rest of the City. Bournville soon attracted interest from other housing reformers and people from all over the world visited the village – it inspired, for instance, developments by Reckitts of Hull and Colmans of Norwich. The Garden City Association paid attention to Bournville when preparing plans for Letchworth. The final accolade came in 1919 when King George V came to the village and left impressed by what he saw.

Over the years the Village Trust has maintained the quality of Bournville as an area in which to live although it has constantly kept up to date and has experimented in such things as solar heating and increasing housing density. Today the village is still a very attractive suburb of Birmingham and retains its 'chocolate box' image, remaining a credit to its creator.

Had the railway not existed at the time the Cadbury brothers were looking for a site to establish their new factory, then it is possible that none of the developments at Bournville would have taken place; indeed, when the village was advertised after it was built, great emphasis was placed on the proximity of the station as a means of travelling to and from work.

FIRST YEARS OF THE TWENTIETH CENTURY

Despite some decline, passenger figures showed something of an upturn in the years immediately following the renaming of the station to 'Bournville' and, by 1907, stood at 155,410, with 449 season ticket holders. In order to retain or even increase the number of passengers, and to compete with developing road transport, plans were made in 1905 to improve arrangements at the station. It was decided to place a booking office, linking the two separate buildings on the 'up' platform and to replace the two separate awnings with a single structure running the full length of the existing buildings and the new booking hall. This new building was to be an extension of the waiting room and all brickwork was to match that already existing, the roof extended in the same slate and hipped style of the

original structure – though there would be two separate pitched roofs divided by a flat roofed toilet block. Access to the platform was by double glazed doors through the waiting room. All was ready during the middle months of 1906. The new platform canopy was a heavy wooden structure, akin to that which had existed before and was similarly supported on simple cast iron brackets. The existing booking hall, at street level, was retained to serve passengers using the 'down' platform, for trains to Kings Norton and destinations further south.

While this work was progressing, there were plans to extend the village at Bournville, which would increase the potential number of passengers. In 1906 an organisation called 'The Bournville Tenants Limited' leased land from the Village Trust and put up a further 398 houses, some self-built, attracting tenants and owners from outside the immediate area. These new occupiers would need public transport to reach their places of employment; many of these new 'immigrants' would use the trams but others would see the railway as a more convenient means of travel.

Cadbury's chocolate factory continued to expand during the early years of the twentieth century, creating further employment and bringing in workers from other parts of Birmingham, some of whom came to the works by train. Freight traffic generated by expanding markets for chocolate went largely by rail, from the company's own system on to the Midland main line. There was also increasing amounts of raw materials and milk. There was also much through freight traffic to and from the Suffolk Street goods depot, although much more of this type of traffic was going via the larger Lawley Street yard. Local 'pick-up' goods trains were running through the station two or three times a day, taking on parcels and other sundries as required.

Another source of traffic for Bournville station was The Works Outing. Along with many other employers at this time, Cadbury hired a train during the summer to take employees for a day at the seaside. It would be made up of rolling stock from the carriage sidings at Kings Norton and a locomotive from Bournville shed. Early on an August morning it would arrive at Bournville station to pick up trippers for a day at either the North Wales coast or the resorts of Somerset and Devon, returning late in the evening. After the First World War these outings were transferred to the roads, using motor coaches.

At the outbreak of World War I, Bournville station saw much traffic serving the expanding village and chocolate factory. The station was an essential component in the development of Bournville and an increasingly useful asset to the Midland Railway. When war was declared, on 4th August 1914, the railways came under Government control. The 'Railway Executive Committee' was created and tried to discourage civilian passenger traffic, with little effect, even though most trains had no restaurant cars, fares increased by 50% up to 1917, and services were drastically cut. There was, however, always a need to run suburban services in order for people to travel to and from their jobs; the Cadbury's workforce was no exception and these trains ran along the BWSR throughout the war. Along with freight traffic for the chocolate factory these formed the lifeblood of Bournville station. Apart from the reduction in express trains passing through, traffic in the immediate area gave the impression that nothing had changed much during the emergency.

Although the Cadbury family were Quakers and against warfare of any sort, their employees were not and there was a rush to join the armed forces as soon as war was declared. The loss of the male workforce to the war effort left the Midland Railway and Cadbury's with a shortage of labour to maintain essential services and production. The railways soon found themselves at full stretch in trying to meet the demands placed on them, moving men and matériel. Cadbury's, bereft of much of the workforce, were also struggling to maintain chocolate production. Industry turned to the largely unused female population, and recruited women to fill their labour needs. For many of these women it was the first time that they had been wage earners in a society where the only place for them was in the home, while others had been in domestic service, working for wealthy families in poor conditions and even worse pay. Women took the chances they were offered and proved to be the equal of men in many of the jobs they did. Thus it was no sur-

prise to see women serving as guards, porters and station staff at Bournville, doing the jobs that only men once did. The railway hardly noticed the difference in operating terms. Although most women returned to domestic life after cessation of hostilities their role would never quite be the same again. As if to highlight this point, their wartime service made female suffrage an inevitability.

The 'War to end all wars' smouldered to its end on 11th November 1918 and with it came an uncertain future, both for the railways and the country as a whole. The war had created men who were adept at handling the internal combustion engine and many redundant motor vehicles were bought up by ex-soldiers. Numbers of them promptly set up in business as road hauliers and motor coach operators, creating future severe competition.

A late nineteenth century view of Cadbury's works, with a train of Midland Railway wagons, hauled by the company's saddle tank loco. (Cadbury Ltd)

Interior of the warehouse at 'Waterside' with Midland Railway open wagons awaiting loading. (Cadbury Ltd)

THE WORKS RAILWAY

Expansion of the chocolate factory over the years meant that the company had to develop an internal transport system within the factory area. It was necessary to connect with the canal and main line railway, for raw materials and fuel into the factory site and the removal of the finished goods. When the factory was first opened, a horse and van sufficed for this work but as it expanded this soon proved unsatisfactory. So the company decided upon its own railway, starting with a small line and exchange sidings alongside the Midland. The lines opened in 1884, operated by a single steam locomotive. As growth continued (factory buildings being added until 1936) the track system developed until a complete railway, totalling six miles, circled the whole manufacturing area. This was achieved by the mid-1920s. A section of the railway crossed the Birmingham West Suburban and the canal over a bridge north of Bournville station, to provide access to warehouses on the far side of the canal, known as 'Waterside'. Sidings were established there, along with a loading area for canal barges.

The railway was built to standard gauge so that there would be no need to unload wagons operating between the main line and the works railway. 'Cadbury's' (as the firm is habitually called) also had its own 'private owner' wagons and vans for coal, coke and chocolate products, the vehicles running directly on and off the main line. From 'Waterside' the railway crossed the overbridge, ran down an incline and around the perimeter of the factory complex. Sidings were placed at convenient points. Connection between the railway and the factory buildings themselves was made by horse and cart, and later fork lift trucks. Some sidings were in fairly confined areas which necessitated some tight curves. These made for a restriction the wheelbases of locomotives, to a maximum of 7ft 6ins. The company also had its own three road engine shed, sited to the north west of the main factory buildings, where the fleet of locomotives could be housed. The number of locomotives steadily increased as the system expanded.

The first was a Peckett 0-4-0 saddle tank with two outside cylinders; the company name CADBURY was carried in brass on the sides of the tank, and it was followed by three further 0-4-0STs, from Dick, Kerr; these had the bold CADBURY again in brass, but were distinguished by additional plates marking them out as No.1, No.2 and No.3. 1 and 2 were purchased in the mid-1890s, and No.3 arrived in 1901. The cabside sheets were lined out, it seems, and the engines were painted a dark red, similar to that used on tins of drinking chocolate, as were all future Cadbury steam engines. The brass then seems to have gone out of fashion and later engines simply carried the words *Cadbury Bournville* - admittedly in a flourish of styling not usually associated with industrial locos. The legend was applied to the tank sides, in gold let-

'Waterside' warehouse, on the opposite bank to Bournville station and Cadbury's works. As well as the Midland to transport its products, Cadbury's also used the Birmingham and Worcester Canal and had interests in the Severn and Canal Carrying Company, whose barges can be seen in this view. Chocolate crumb was carried by Charlie Atkins (Chocolate Charlie) in this boat, 'Mendip', until 1961. Children of boat operators were always treated to chocolate by Cadbury's, which they, no doubt, missed when this trade ceased. (Cadbury Ltd)

Cadbury employees unloading milk churns from Midland Railway vans onto carts for onward transit into the works. The loco in charge is 0-4-0 saddle tank No.3. (Cadbury Ltd)

Cadbury No.6 is reflected in the water of the Birmingham and Worcester Canal as it rests at 'Waterside'. (R.C. Riley)

tering with full lining around the tank edges, cabs and backs.

With the exception of HOLLYMOOR, a Manning Wardle 0-6-0ST obtained from the Austin Motor Co. (and probably used on construction work, according to the *Industrial Railway Handbook*, from which these details are culled) subsequent engines were all 0-4-0s. No.4, No.5 and No.6 were Avonside 0-4-0 side tanks of 1910, 1913 and 1923 respectively. With the first CADBURY No.1 scrapped, a new Avonside, an 0-4-0T of 1925, became No.1. Characteristic of the Avonsides were tanks running the full length of the boiler and smokebox, set above a short wheelbase. The whole was thoroughly reminiscent of the '1101' class engines built for the GWR. The Cadbury Avonsides had fully enclosed backs with rectangular windows and screens. Front windows were also rectangular and opened outwards.

After the Avonsides there was then a gap until the 1940s, when a second-hand Peckett 0-4-0ST arrived. It took No.8 in the Cadbury scheme of things. No.9 was an 0-4-0T from Hunslet, arriving in 1949, followed by another Peckett 0-4-0ST, No.10, in 1955. No.9 had some

obvious differences from the others, in that its side tanks did not extend for the whole length of the boiler. Other differences were a flat topped dome which contained safety valve and whistle, round windows front and back, and a small bunker behind the cab. Other dimensions were similar to the rest of the fleet. No.9 featured in a film made by the company in the 1950s about Bournville, the works and the village. No.9 was later scrapped at Bournville (see below) while No.10 went to the National Coal Board after its Cadbury service.

In the early 1950s all steam engines were converted from coal to coke firing in order to reduce the smoke problem. Being a food factory, this was deemed specially important. The higher heat generated with coke meant that copper tubes in the boilers had to be replaced by steel examples. No.10 was built to burn coke from new.

1958 saw the beginning of the end for steam at the works with the delivery of the first diesel, No.11. No. 14 was the last to be delivered (in 1961) and like the other diesels, Nos.11, 12 (of 1959), and 13 (of 1961), was a North British 0-4-0, with hydraulic transmission. This new form of motive power made the steam fleet redundant,

although No.9 was retained as standby in case of diesel failures or increased demand for motive power. It eventually went for scrap in 1966. Steam No.1 was given by the company to the Dowty Railway Preservation people in 1963, on condition that the Cadbury livery was retained. It was removed to the Dowty site at Ashchurch, keeping company with 46201 PRINCESS ELIZABETH, the ex-LMS Pacific. This was to be the start of a much travelled life for the engine.

No.1 stayed at Ashchurch until 1983, when it was moved to Toddington, home of the Gloucestershire and Warwickshire Railway, after the Dowty Preservation Group had to vacate their premises. At Toddington the loco worked passenger services (a new role) from 1984 to 1986. In 1988 No.1 was bought by the Birmingham Railway Museum, Tyseley, with financial help from Cadbury's which wished to see the engine return to the Birmingham area. On its way to Tyseley No.1 paid a brief visit to its original home at Bournville, on November 3rd.

The Cadbury rolling stock consisted of four wheeled coal and coke wagons of between 8 and 12 tons. The 8 ton wagons were of 7 plank timber construction, the rest steel. The

Cadbury No.10 0-4-0 saddle tank, built by Pecketts of Bristol in 1955. This engine was designed to burn coke from new, the others having been converted to coke a few years previously, in an effort to maintain a cleaner environment, so important to the food industry. (R.C. Riley)

wooden wagons had single dropside doors, while the steel ones had double side opening doors. The 10 ton vehicles had one pair and the 12 tonners two pairs. All of them were built by the Birmingham Wagon Company and were lettered 'Cadbury, Bournville' on the sides with the wagon number in the bottom left corner. Once steam traction had finished on the company's railway, all of these wagons went for scrap.

Cadbury also owned several four wheeled vans, both for internal and external use. All were of wood and steel construction with central sliding doors and painted brown or grey – later ones had the 'Cadbury' logo and place of origin painted in white at the top of one end of the vehicle with its stock number at the lower opposite end. Many of these vans had been purchased from the old main line companies. Four, preserved on the Severn Valley Railway since August 1967, were originally owned by the Caledonian Railway, probably built by Cravens of Sheffield between 1918 and 1922. When the internal railway system closed, remaining Cadbury's vans were scrapped.

After World War II there was a steadily increasing trend to roads for the movement of goods and Cadbury's were no exception to this. By the mid-1950s the company was running an extensive fleet of road vans. The company ceased using the Birmingham and Worcester Canal in 1964. The railway was becoming less useful for internal movement; road vehicles were more flexible in use and could gain access to parts of the factory that the railway could not. By 1976, 90% of all goods to and from the factory were travelling by road, using freightliners and containers.

Maintenance costs involved in running the railway were becoming prohibitive by this time and there was also a steep decline in the number of customers who themselves had rail links. All of these factors combined to force the closure of the railway. The last trains ran in May 1976 and over the next few months all remaining locos were sold off and the track torn up, the railway becoming just a memory after an existence of 92 years. Diesel No. 14 was preserved on the Llangollen Railway but has now returned to Cadburys works as a static exhibit.

In its heyday well over three quarters of all Cadbury's traffic had been moved using the railway. Three trains a day of up to 60 vans full of finished chocolate products were hauled up the incline to connect with the BWSR – all of this would now have to go by road. Industrial railways were falling out of use in many parts of Britain at this time. Cadbury was no exception and it is pleasing that at least one of its locos has been preserved to remind us of the great days of the system around Bournville works.

THE GROUPING YEARS

The turbulent years between the two World Wars were marked, initially, by industrial unrest, which culminated in the General Strike of 1926 and the Great Depression which reached its peak in 1931. These years had a profound effect on the railways in terms of severe road competition and extensive reorganisation. Industrial relations had been strained in the years prior to the First World War, marked by several major strikes, but industrial disputes were largely suspended for the duration of the emergency. When peace returned and the 'Land fit for Heroes' turned out somewhat short of the promise, the old grievances began to reappear on the heels of wage stagnation, despite an economic 'boom' and price increases. The railways were hit by a national strike in 1919, which brought the whole network to a standstill, the same year that Bournville station played host to King George V on his visit to George Cadbury's Model Village. The strike forced the travelling public to seek alternatives and they turned to the roads. In Birmingham the tram system was well developed and commuters to and from Bournville travelled to work by tram, and many continued to do so after the rail strike was settled, a loss of revenue to the BWSR. For longer journeys, the new motor coaches were becoming an attractive alternative to the railways as they could offer more of a door to door service, which went someway to compensating for longer journey times. Various miners strikes in this period affected coal supplies to the railways causing difficulties in maintaining services.

By far the greatest threat to the railways was the now booming demand for private cars. One impetus for this demand was the development of the 'Baby Austin Seven' at nearby Longbridge. The car was designed by Herbert Austin in six months and introduced in 1922 at a purchase price of £168. The significance of this car was not really apparent when it was first introduced, the public was used to larger vehicles and ridiculed the 'Baby Austin' until a Cambridge undergraduate an-

Cadbury No.9 loco outside the shed in March 1955. (Roger Carpenter Collection)

Cadbury No.1 an Avonside built loco, outside the locoshed in March 1955. (Roger Carpenter Collection)

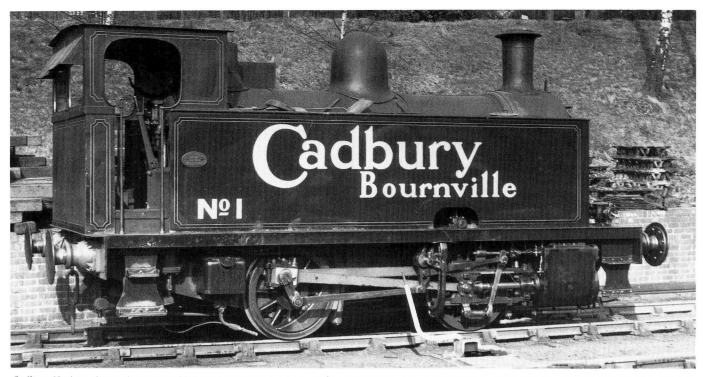

Cadbury No.1 on the works railway. This loco was withdrawn in 1963, when replaced by diesel traction, and found its way into preservation. She can now be seen at the Birmingham Railway Museum, Tyseley. (R.C. Riley)

nounced in *The Times* that he was going to purchase one. This gave the car instant 'snob' appeal and it became a great success, bringing the prospect of 'mass motoring' to the British population. Motor cycle and bicycle production also boomed in immediate post-war Birmingham with companies like BSA, Velocette and Ariel increasing production to meet public demand.

The railways themselves were retained under Government control until 15th August 1921. After which compensation was paid for abnormal maintenance costs incurred as a result of wartime traffic demands. Compensa-

tion was slow in being paid but, eventually, £60 million was allocated to the railways for necessary restoration and repair work. The 'Grouping' to create four massive organisations from the myriad railway companies took effect from 1st January 1923. The Midland lost its individual identity to the London Midland and Scottish Railway Company. Bournville station became part of the LMS at the grouping, along with the rest of the Birmingham West Suburban Railway.

Following the grouping, the LMS embarked upon a series of modernisation programmes, updating and improving its existing

buildings. Bournville station benefitted from this by having the waiting shelter on the 'down' platform demolished and replaced by a more substantial structure, extending from the top of the subway staircase to the point where the old one had existed. The subway itself was taken out of use and a new one, placed further inside the street level station concourse, was opened.

As far as trains were concerned, the new company retained local services, running as many as the old Midland had done. Expresses were augmented by the introduction in 1927 of two new named trains, using the Birming-

Cadbury No.10 rests from her labours during the 1950s. (R.C. Riley)

ham Suburban and passing through Bournville station, the 'Devonian' and the 'Pines Express'. The remainder of the 1920s and 1930s was marked by the Great Depression and high unemployment in Britain. Birmingham was not as badly hit as the North of England, Wales and Scotland and employment levels were maintained at Cadbury's. In fact at this time, working at Bournville, much like the railways, appeared to guarantee a certain amount of job security. Down the road at Longbridge, the Austin Motor Works continued to turn out its vehicles for a 'well heeled' market. Local trains continued to be used and services survived. In the 'peak' evening hours, five trains left Longbridge taking Austin employees to their homes, some using the BWSR and calling at Bournville station.

As if to emphasise their confidence in the future, Cadbury's opened their factory to the public in the 1930s. This attracted much interest and tours were arranged from many parts of the country. Most of these visitors came to Bournville by rail, visitors from London came to Bournville from Euston via the LNWR line to Birmingham, using the BWSR from there. On more than one occasion the train returned in the southbound direction, ran around the Lifford Loop and passed through Bournville station again, much to the surprise of the passengers.

While these Cadbury's excursions brought in welcome revenue, pressure from road transport forced the LMS to revise its fare structures. Low fares were introduced on long distance trains and 'save to travel' schemes were introduced in 1936, offering a halfpenny interest per month for every ten shillings saved. By 1938, around 85% of passenger receipts were derived from low fares compared to 34·4% in 1924. At Bournville some of the deals offered included tickets which allowed passengers to catch expresses to Bristol from New Street and included free travel on local services in order to meet these expresses. This applied at all stations to Barnt Green where the expresses did not stop. Another offer was a cheap (6d) return from New Street and all stations, including Bournville, to Barnt Green. These were valid on weekday evenings, Saturday afternoons, and all day Sunday. Barnt Green station is the gateway to the Lickey Hills, a local beauty spot well visited by Brummies and these tickets proved very popular on summer Sunday afternoons. As if to predict future trends, however, the competing tram from Birmingham City centre, along the A38 Bristol Road to the Lickey Hills was more popular than the trains. The train fare itself was increased to 6½d during the summer of 1939, immediately prior to the outbreak of World War II.

WORLD WAR II AND NATIONALISATION

When the Prime Minister, Birmingham's own Neville Chamberlain, announced to the nation, on Sunday 3rd September 1939, that Britain was at war with Germany, plans had already been made to bring the railways under Government control in much the same way as they had been during the Great War. Conflict had seemed inevitable as early as 1937, inducing the Government to make preparations for the takeover. Plans were in place by 1938. By 1st September 1939 the crisis had deepened sufficiently for these to be put into effect and the railways came under State control.

The Spanish Civil War had shown that the bombing of open towns and cities was almost inevitable. Birmingham, as the industrial centre of England, would be a prime target, and this was recognised when evacuation plans were drawn up. Children from all over the City were moved out, Bournville station playing its part in the process. On the face of it, Bournville would have seemed a very safe area, with industry of little strategic importance to an enemy, but it was surrounded by engineering works at Selly Oak, Stirchley and Longbridge, making the whole area vulnerable. The Cadbury works, moreover, would have looked the same as any

Cadbury No.10 shunts the company's vans outside the 'Waterside' warehouse in March 1955, shortly after arriving from her builders. (Roger Carpenter Collection)

Cadbury No.1 on the works railway in the 1950s. (R.C. Riley)

No.1 poses for photographers during an open day in 1955. (R.C. Riley)

factory from the air, despite its (ostensibly – see later) non-strategic nature. With this in mind, children from Bournville were evacuated through the station to Gloucestershire and those rural parts of South Wales served by the LMS, avoiding a busy New Street station and the City centre.

Bournville saw fewer trains during this period as Government policy began to bite. Military traffic including ambulance trains from the South Coast ports to New Street, and trains to supply the armed forces with munitions produced in the factories of Birmingham and the 'Black Country' all passed along the BWSR and through Bournville station. War also brought women back into the workforce to replace men who had been conscripted into the forces, for there was no rush to volunteer as there had been in 1914. Women have largely remained a major part of the labour market since and have not been banished to the 'kitchen sink' as they had after the First World War, mainly because the post-war 'consumer boom' required a female labour force (at lower rates) for the more intricate assembly work. Women and the BWSR at Bournville were to become increasingly important during the war years as part of the Cadbury factory was turned over to munitions production. As men were called up for the forces, their jobs were taken over by women, encouraged by the Government as part of the war effort. A section of the chocolate works became a 'shadow factory' and was renamed Bournville Utilities Limited, going to war producing hand grenades, gas masks, very lights and aircraft parts for Boulton and Paul. Those who worked on munitions were retained on Cadbury's payroll. The remaining parts of the factory still turned out chocolate and cocoa, principally for soldiers' rations, even though newspaper advertisements at that time gave the impression that none was being produced. All of this of course brought increasing levels of traffic to Bournville station; suburban traffic was largely unaffected by the war as these trains were run for 'essential workers'

The raids of 1940/1 affected Birmingham as much as any other major city; most of the centre was damaged and the ex-LNWR side of New Street station roof destroyed. Bournville did not escape, though the factory, station and railway remained unscathed throughout the war. The only damage in the area was to the bridge carrying Cadbury's private railway over the Birmingham and Worcester canal, when it was bombed on the night of 19th November 1940.

The war years brought some unusual motive power to the BSWR and on trains passing through Bournville. In 1942-43, ex-LSWR S11 4-4-0s were loaned the the LMS and were often to be seen on trains worked from the Somerset and Dorset through to New Street. Around the same time, ex-LNWR 'George V' and 'Precursor' 4-4-0s were regularly seen on troop trains between Birmingham and Bristol,

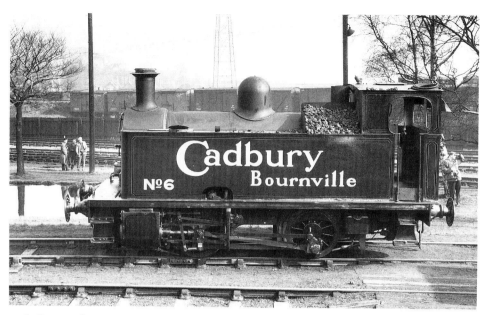

Cadbury No.6 on the works railway. (R.C. Riley).

Cadbury No.6 rests on 4th March 1961. (J. Peden)

The shed for Cadbury locos as it appeared in March 1955. Loco No.5 is in the foreground, with No.1 in the distance. (Roger Carpenter Collection)

Cadbury No.6 outside the locoshed. Just in view is replacement traction in the form of diesel locomotive No.12. (R.C. Riley)

this at a time when they had long disappeared from the old LNW system around Birmingham. In 1944, LNER B12 4-6-0s sometimes worked ambulance trains to New Street. There was even a working to Bristol using B12 No. 8549, piloted by ex-LSWR S11 No.-401, then allocated to Saltley. Other types seen in the locality during this period included Stanier 8F and US Army S160 2-8-0s, WD 2-8-0s and 2-10-0s.

When war was finally over in Europe in May 1945, traffic along the BWSR gradually returned to something like normal. Expresses from the north to Bristol were resumed, although at nothing like their pre-war speeds. Inadequate maintenance on the railway during the war had seen to that. The LMS calculated that it would cost £26 million to bring the track throughout its system back up to the standard that it was in 1939, let alone another

£4 million just to complete arrears of repairs built up during the six years of war. The Government had promised, in 1940, that the railways would not lose out on revenue earned during the conflict; in the event, it welched on the deal and paid out less than half of the earnings during that period.

The railway companies had been very short of money at the outbreak of war because of the effects of the Great Depression, road competition and fare reductions made to attract passengers. The LMS had not been able to pay a dividend since 1938. All of this combined to make the recovery rate very slow for the railways, for they had to bear the costs of repairing enemy damage themselves as well as try to restore worn out equipment. They could not even expect help from the Treasury for the system was at least usable, unlike that in most of Europe.

Cadbury's returned to chocolate production after the war, although cocoa would be in short supply until the early 1950s and its products rationed until 1953. There was a lack of 'hard currency' because of the costs of the war which made the import of cocoa very difficult and Government policy was to export as much as possible – importation was officially discouraged. Employment did not diminish in this period as the reconstruction and export 'boom' required as much labour as possible, particularly at Austin at Longbridge. High employment meant that BWSR suburban services remained at pre-war levels, an all day hourly train calling at Bournville, supplemented by extra trains at morning and evening 'peak hours'. The BWSR provided the only suburban service to south west Birmingham stations after the closure of the Camp Hill branch to passengers in 1946.

Locos Nos 10, 1 and 6 are posed together in this view of 4th March 1961. (J. Peden)

The end of the war was marked by calls for Nationalisation of key industries, as there had been in 1918. There was also a sense of unity felt by the people, engendered by six years of war, which led to the wish for a 'better world'. These ideas were brought to fruition with the election of a Labour Government, under Clement Attlee, by a landslide in 1945. The new Government established a policy which would introduce the Welfare State, its main plank being the National Health Service, and nationalisation of major industries such as mining and the railways. While the railway companies tried to resist, rank and file railwaymen saw it as salvation. In the end the railway company's efforts came to nothing.

The 1947 Transport Act which embodied nationalisation of railways and road transport, envisaged an integrated system. The railways would become the main carriers with buses and lorries acting as feeders, a situation that would have proved very useful during the oil crisis of the 1970s, and may well have prevented the road congestion so common in the 1980s. The Government had clearly recognised the growing importance of the roads and chose to have an integrated system rather than road and rail in destructive competition with one another. In the years immediately following the war and the lack of currency to import oil, this was probably a very sensible idea.

At nationalisation Bournville station ceased to be part of the London, Midland and Scottish Railway and became a station on the Western Region of British Railways, although it reverted back to the London Midland Region in 1958. The station was now part of a State owned railway system. Having survived the war virtually unscathed its future prospects looked very bright indeed, with traffic remaining at the high levels that they had been in the past. Changes were, however, on the way and Bournville would not come through them without some alterations.

BOURNVILLE ENGINE SHED

Bournville shed was situated a little south of the station, alongside the junction of the Birmingham West Suburban line to Kings Norton and the branch to Lifford. Opened in 1895 it was the standard roundhouse type and one of the last built by the Midland. Coded 3a, its purpose was to supply motive power for an expected rise in traffic on the BWSR. This never really materialised. When opened, the shed was supplied with a 50ft. turntable, enlarged to 57ft. in 1948, and a single coaling stage. The shed housed around twenty five locos as an outstation of Saltley, Birmingham.

By 1929 there were only seventeen engines – a pair of 4-4-0s; four 2-4-0s; half a dozen 0-6-0s; two Johnson 1F 0-6-0 tanks and three Deeley 0-6-4 tanks. The 0-6-4Ts, known as 'flatirons' by the locomotive crews, had been on local suburban services until 1924, and some had even been used on Birmingham – Leicester expresses until they experienced a number of derailments. Six were then tried on the Tilbury line in Essex, but the locos were downgraded and eventually withdrawn, several being stored at the side of the shed. Many other withdrawn locos were stored at Bournville over the years, including ex-LNWR 18 inch goods 4-6-0s.

The Bournville complement did increase to twenty nine in 1945, the stock being three Stanier 3MT 2-6-2 tanks; two Midland 2P 4-4-0s; four LMS 4P 4-4-0 Compounds; one Midland 1F 0-6-0 tank; six Midland 3F 0-6-0s;

Bournville roundhouse from a passing train on 1st June 1957. Several of the small 2F and 3F 0-6-0 goods tender engines, of ex-Midland design, populate the area. In the right background is Bournville signalbox. (N.E. Preedy)

two LMS 4F 0-6-0s; six Midland double framed 2F 0-6-0s; three Fowler 4MT 2-6-4 tanks and one Stanier 4MT 2-6-4 tank. These latter four engines were introduced to the shed for local suburban services. The LMS did not modernise the shed under its renewal programme of the 1930s although a mobile canteen, presented by men of the Argentine Railway, was put up inside the roundhouse itself. The shed was recoded 21B in 1935, marking it, under a new scheme designed to yield efficiencies in engine working and maintenance, a 'garage' of Saltley (21A). Apparently there was a very strict shedmaster at Bournville at this time who did not like strangers around the area. Anyone caught without permission was summarily ejected.

From the mid-1930s the shed became even more of a backwater, and declined further when suburban services ceased on the Camp Hill line. Many elderly engines could be found there, including a number of Kirtley double framed 0-6-0s retained for the Halesowen branch (opened September 10th 1883 and closed June 6th 1964); its Dowry Dell viaduct could not bear engines heavier than a 2F 0-6-0. The last to remain on shed, No. 22846, was not withdrawn until 1949. Even

in the late 1950s there was still a number of old engines at Bournville. I well remember, as a child trainspotter at Kings Norton, an ancient Midland 2F 0-6-0 on shunting duties, as late as 1959.

The number of locos stabled at Bournville increased to thirty one in 1950, after nationalisation, and included two 3MT 2-6-2 tanks; two 2P 4-4-0s; four 4P 4-4-0s; five 4MT 2-6-4 tanks; eight 3F 0-6-0s; three 4F 0-6-0s; four 'Black 5' 4-6-0s and three 2F 0-6-0s. The 2Ps and 2Fs dated back to the latter end of the nineteenth century. The shed was put out of action for a short while in 1956 when an engine fell into a pit, damaging the turntable which was sent to Swindon for repair. All locos then had to go to Saltley or Bromsgrove for boiler inspections and washouts. This mishap boded ill for the shed and it was scheduled for closure in 1959, when the allocation was down to twenty two locos. At this time, no tanks were used on suburban services, which were usually entrusted to 4Fs, Class 5s and Ivatt Class 4s. In the event, Bournville survived until 14th February 1960 with 'Black 5' No. 44843 the last engine off shed. Remaining in store were 2P 4-4-0s Nos. 40439, 40443, 40511 and 40568 along with 3F 0-6-0s

Nos. 43490, 43675, 43858, 44084, 44227, 44406 and 44515. These were all removed shortly afterwards. The 2Ps went to Toton and finished their time on freight workings up to January 1961. The whole site was cleared and is now occupied by modern industrial units.

The shed existed for 65 years which was a long life when one considers its insignificance within the main railway network. It was never fully utilised once it was realised that traffic along the Birmingham West Suburban line was not going to be as good as had been hoped. It became a quiet place indeed, almost a retirement home for engines not required elsewhere – a mecca for railway enthusiasts. It could be argued that through lack of modernisation to the shed, and the elderly engines housed there, Bournville became something of a living museum, giving some idea of what a working nineteenth century loco shed was like, well into the 1950s.

THE FIFTIES

The 1950s were marked by the continuing 'consumer boom' and the Suez Crisis, both of which had a marked effect on the BWSR and Bournville station, increasing freight and

Bournville shed from the Lifford branch. The Lifford branch went out of use when the Camp Hill line was closed to suburban traffic, as a wartime measure, on 27th January 1941. (D. Ibbotson)

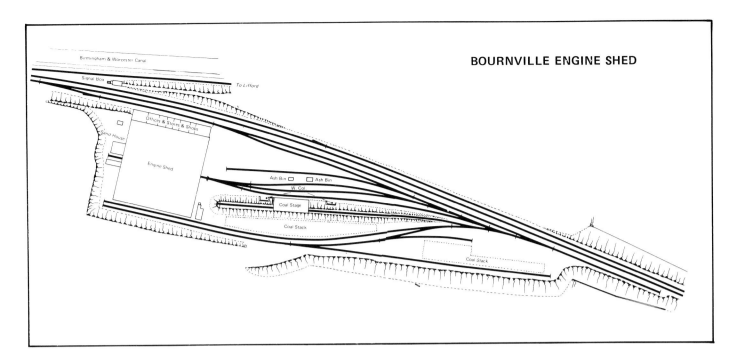

BOURNVILLE ENGINE SHED

One of the picturesque double-framed Kirtley 0-6-0 gods engines, LMS No.2603, near the coaling stage at Bournville shed on 2nd March 1935. These old Midland Railway engines had a long life at Bournville, being of a sufficiently light weight to be used over the Dowry Dell viaduct on the Halesowen branch, where engines no heavier than 2F classification could be used. (H.C. Casserley)

passenger traffic in the area. By the end of the decade, however, the development of cheap motoring along with expanding lorry fleets, appeared to signal the demise of Britain's railways. Lifting of import restrictions on cocoa allowed Cadbury's to prosper during the early 1950s. From this point, the company enjoyed its most successful period since the introduction of 'Dairy Milk' chocolate in 1905. At the same time, the firm gained a 'high profile' image in public relations. From 1950 until 1970, the year after they merged with Schweppes, Cadbury's welcomed an average 100,000 visitors a year to Bournville. Special excursion trains were laid on from all over Britain to reveal the mysteries of Easter eggs, choc bars and the rest.

Bournville station and the BWSR did not seem to be greatly affected during this period, there were still the same number of commuter trains operating, although some of these were in the hands of diesel multiple units as the Modernization Plan began to take effect. Express trains passed through Bournville at a similar rate, and even increased during the summer, some in the hands of new 'Peak' Type 4 diesels. Freight traffic to Cadbury's did decrease over the decade, but the retention of the private railway by the company ensured that some goods were still carried by rail. Though goods traffic was increasingly going via Lawley Street at the expense of Suffolk Street, as road competition began to bite, causing loss of this traffic on the BWSR. By the end of the decade, very little through goods traffic passed Bournville station. A good many visitors to the works travelled to Bournville by motor coach and these numbers increased in the 1960s.

The decade ended with road transport having greater than ever influence; by 1960 the Macmillan Government called a halt to the increasingly expensive Modernization Plan and at the same time, the Minister of Transport, Ernest Marples, appointed an advisory group, led by Sir Ian Stedeford, to look at the administration of BR in an effort to find a better management approach. A member of this group was to have a major influence on the railway system in the following decade. His name was Dr. (later Lord) Richard Beeching who became Chairman of the British Railways Board.

Dr. Beeching published his 'Reshaping Report of British Railways' in the spring of 1963, advocating the closure of over 5000 route miles of railway, and 2350 stations as hopelessly uneconomic. Bournville station and the BWSR were not included. Reasons for this were that the report considered that suburban services in the major cities should be retained because the pattern of life required them, although these trains should 'not run below cost'. This suggested heavy fare increases unless subsidies were retained. Modified services between New Street, Redditch and Barnt Green were suggested, perhaps 'peak hour' traffic only. The tone of the report did, however, mean that Bournville station would still be required.

The BWSR was always safe from closure as one of the main routes from Birmingham to the West Country. Its position was further strengthened even before the publication of the 'Reshaping Report' when all South West and South Wales trains, including ex-GWR and Western Region express 'The Cornishman', were transferred from the Birmingham and North Warwick Line via Stratford-on-Avon to the Birmingham and Gloucester line (using the BWSR) on 10th September 1962. Dieselisation under the Modernization Plan allowed the elimination of banking assistance at the Lickey incline and offered the prospect of immediate development of the Derby to Bristol trunk route, which included the BWSR. This involved concentration of North East to South West traffic. the reasons behind this were detailed in the British Railways Board plan of February 1965, 'The Development of Major Railway Trunk Routes' – it showed that the line between Birmingham and Gloucester carried by far the heaviest freight traffic between the West Midlands, South Wales, and the South West of England; 90,000 tons per week, compared with 70,000 tons on the Worcester and Hereford line, and 60,000 tons via Stratford-on-Avon and Gloucester. Future traffic flows estimated 45 trains a day between the West Midlands and Bristol with a similar number to South Wales. Line capacity was calculated at approximately 140 trains a day running at speeds of between 35 and 70 miles per hour. Concentration on one line was expected to produce large savings in running costs. This was achieved in 1965 and allowed closure of the Stratford-on-Avon and Midland Junction line, which had been an important by-pass route, avoiding the congested West Midlands during World War II, for mineral traffic to and from South Wales. Next to go was the Shrewsbury and Hereford route, in 1973, its expresses being diverted via Birmingham, using the BWSR to gain access to New Street. New Street station itself had been completely rebuilt as part of a major electrification scheme between London and Crewe in 1964, all London trains running via Birmingham Snow Hill until the work had been completed. Local traffic using the BWSR continued to have access to New Street as rebuilding was carried on. As more traffic was concentrated on the Derby to Bristol line, via the BWSR, Bournville station saw increasing rail activity.

Bournville shed was used as a storage area for withdrawn locomotives from other areas. Here, ex-Lancs and Yorks Aspinall 0-6-0 goods engines Nos. 12114, 12106 and 12137 await their fate on 2nd March 1935. (H.C. Casserley)

Major setbacks were encountered, including closure of the Suffolk Street goods depot in March 1967, with freight being concentrated at Lawley Street, those trains using the Camp Hill branch. The only freights on the BWSR after this were Cadbury's and through freights via New Street. Closure of the Halesowen branch, in June 1964, meant that the station lost some suburban work, particularly 'peak hour' trains to the Austin works at Longbridge.

On the face of it, Bournville station, along with the rest of the BWSR looked relatively secure with plenty of traffic both calling and passing through and Beeching's proposals offering little threat. However, industrial relations, particularly in the motor industry, were deteriorating with strikes called in pursuit of higher pay. The 1960s also saw warnings that the industries of Birmingham were too reliant on an increasingly uncompetitive motor industry. By the end of that decade, virtually all of the motor cycle industry had disappeared in the face of Japanese competition and there were lay offs in other, linked, industries. At the end of the 1960s unemployment increased sharply with levels rising to above the national average for the first time. With unemployment rising, the need for public transport declined causing a general reduction in rail traffic and a real threat to suburban services, the lifeblood of Bournville station, in the Birmingham area.

RECESSION

Unemployment and the spread of roads and motorways were important features of the 1970s in Birmingham, both were to have serious short term consequences for Bournville station and the railways of the city. Unemployment continued to rise throughout the decade as the traditional metal based industries were hit by bankruptcies and loss of markets. Perhaps the most potent symbol of decline was the closure of Snow Hill station on 4th March 1972.

On the BWSR by 1973 there were only two trains each way per day, plus 'peak hour' services, calling at Bournville station. Passenger numbers continued to decline and, as if to reflect this, only two stations remained open, downgraded to unmanned halts – Bournville and Selly Oak. Both served important industrial locations, which probably saved them. Bournville itself lost all freight traffic when Cadbury's closed its own railway in May 1976, and no goods traffic has used the BWSR since. The future for suburban services began to look extremely bleak by this time, but plans were being put forward to improve the situation within the next few years.

Consultants had reported in 1971, suggesting a rapid transit system along the 'A38 Corridor' from Longbridge to Four Oaks, near Sutton Coldfield, utilising the BWSR and Lichfield branches, with a three mile underground link between Aston and the University. The cost was estimated at around £50 million, with an extra £6 million for an extension to Redditch New Town. These consultants considered that the commuter system in Birmingham needed pulling together and streamlining. This report came at a time when Manchester was considering something similar and Liverpool was about to extend its Merseyrail underground system.

The West Midlands Passenger Transport Executive, which had been formed under the terms of the 1968 Transport Act was responsible for municipal bus services and their integration. They also contracted local railway services from BR, who ran them, but the PTE were responsible for incurred losses. Central Government offered all PTE's 75% infrastructure grants towards redevelopment costs of approved transport schemes. The consultant's report was greeted with enthusiasm by the WMPTE and plans were drawn up for development of a Cross City Line from Four Oaks to Longbridge, using the old LNWR line to Lichfield and the Midland line to Bristol, including the BWSR. The project was fully approved under the grant scheme. A new station at Longbridge would replace the one that had existed on the closed Halesowen branch, although it would be situated behind the motor car factory, about a mile distant from the original, close to the front of the factory. Construction of new stations and refurbishment of existing ones were put out to tender.

Work on the BWSR included new station buildings at Five Ways and University with station refurbishment at Selly Oak, Bournville and Kings Norton. 'University' had never existed before and was built to serve the Birmingham University campus at Bournbrook, more directly than from nearby Selly Oak. The contract for all this was awarded to Bullock Construction Ltd. of Aldridge, Staffordshire who had estimated the cost at £462,670, work commencing on 13th December 1976. The tender values for Bournville station were £34,307, made up of £16,097 for a street level ticket office and £18,210 for work on the main station buildings. The whole contract was complete on 31st March 1978 at a total cost of £576,522. All of these stations had similar 1970s architecture and all were decorated in WMPTE colour schemes.

Ex-Midland Railway Johnson 0-6-0 goods loco rests at the side of the locoshed on 9th May 1936. (H.C. Casserley)

29

CADBURY'S COCOA

"CADBURYS" - The Good Old English Cocoa
of the Good Old English Days.

STILL THE BEST TODAY.

A rear view of the preserved Cadbury No.1 0-4-0 on the works railway. (R.C. Riley)

Once the work was complete, the Transport Executive ran intensive services between Four Oaks and Longbridge in a bid to attract passengers away from the roads, encouraging them to leave their cars at home. Trains were calling at Bournville every fifteen minutes each way, some going through to Redditch or Lichfield. An hourly service was run on a Sunday, useful for visitors to the Lickey Hills during the summer months. These services were a great success and were very popular with commuters working in the centre of Birmingham, as they could avoid traffic problems associated with the city's roads during 'peak hours'. All of which suggests that the public will use the railways if a good service is provided. As the recession faded, the Cross-City service became heavily used, bringing its own problems, for it became a victim of its own success. Passenger figures reached £10 million a year in 1990, representing around 30,000 journeys a day.

As manufacturing declined in Birmingham, the city turned to the service industries, in the shape of tourism, conference centres and hotels. A steam railway centre had already been established at Tyseley in 1969 and

the city opened up its canals to tourism during the 1970s, restoring banks, towpaths and locks; allowing them to be used for boating, walking and other leisure activities. After all, Birmingham can boast more miles of canal then Venice. New conference centres and hotels were built, mainly to serve the National Exhibition Centre, opened by the Queen in February 1976. By the mid-1980s, all of this effort had created a new economic 'boom' for the city and brought much new employment, with consequent increased demand for the road network and public transport system. The Cross-City railway line benefitted greatly from this as those employed in the new service industries looked to the trains as a means of going to work, and thereby avoiding the overcrowded roads. During the 1980s the Cross-City service became the busiest commuter line outside London. Unfortunately British Rail persisted in using life-expired diesel multiple units, unreliable and prone to breakdown.

The local press took up the complaints of passengers, the 'Sunday Mercury' featuring a series of articles and editorials on the problems of the Cross-City service. One item, reported

on 21st January 1990, highlighted increasing chaos, and even reported that the train drivers themselves could not arrive at work on time to take their own trains out because of the failure of earlier ones, causing a 'knock-on' effect with later trains not running through the absence of drivers. The 'Sunday Mercury' echoed the feelings of many when it called for electrification, with new rolling stock. In the event the Secretary of State for Transport announced, on 7th February 1990, that the 32 miles of the Cross-City service, including Bournville, is to be electrified at a cost of £18 million, covering new track, overhead power cables and the raising of bridges, the work to be completed by 1993. New rolling stock, in the form of three car electric units costing another £18 million, were ordered on 26th July 1990, when contracts were signed with Hunslet for new class 323 sets, with a seating capacity of 289 and an improved degree of passenger comfort. Construction commenced early in 1991. Increased acceleration associated with electric traction should reduce full journey times by 16 minutes.

Increasing use of the Cross-City service and its electrification will assure the future of

Bournville station for many years to come. Its position has been further secured with the opening, in 1990, of a museum of chocolate. Known as *Cadbury World*, this unusual museum is situated in the original factory site at Bournville and is expected to attract around 250,000 visitors a year. Some of them will almost certainly arrive by train, to Bournville station, in much the same way as those who had first come to marvel at the factory, in the years when it was open to the public. With the opening of Cadbury World, Bournville station was repainted in 'Cadbury Purple' with the firm's 'Glass and a Half' symbol attached to the platform fence, and a board advertising the museum.

If you have been to the works in the past, or if you have visited the new museum, perhaps this book will have helped you consider the past and continuing importance of the Birmingham West Suburban line, and Bournville station, in the social and economic evolution of this small district of Birmingham.

A local passenger train, headed (top) by ex-LMS 4F 0-6-0 No. 43911, pauses at Bournville station, in August 1959. (Gordon Coltas). The lower picture shows Bournville station as it appeared in the late 1950s. To the right a local goods is shunting. The old station building was demolished in 1977 to make way for a new structure as part of development of the BWSR for the new cross-city service. (Lens of Sutton)

ACKNOWLEDGEMENTS

I should like to record my thanks to those people and organisations without whose assistance this book would not have been written. Special thanks go to Helen M. Davies, of the Library and Archive Department at Cadbury Limited, who patiently dealt with my many queries; Mrs. C. A. Turton, Community Officer, Bournville Village Trust, who supplied much detail on the village; Mr. K. R. Maxwell, Regional Quantity Surveyor, Bullock Construction Limited, who provided details on the rebuilding of Bournville station during the 1970s. Other queries were patiently dealt with by Mr. Patrick Baird, Head of Local Studies at the Birmingham Reference Library, the Birmingham Post and Mail, British Rail, Birmingham and the National Railway Museum. Individual assistance was provided by Mr. Arthur Truby, Roger Carpenter, Marjorie Ridgewell and Beatrice Bowerman. I should also like to thank those who provided the photographs used in this work. Finally thanks to my wife, Alwen, who has shown much patience as I have pursued my interest in railways.